I0448039

Understanding
The Political Class

Douglas A. Nagan

Understanding the Political Class

ISBN: 1502825716
ISBN-13:978 1502825711

DEDICATION

To my grandchildren. In the hope that they will have a better informed perspective on the political class[1]. My hope is that this perspective will provide awareness and some protection against the foolishness and inanities the political class will inflict on them and their fellow citizens.

Why do this? Because today's schools and media do not seem to provide civic history, perspective, or understanding regarding current events, our country and form of government. They seem to work on indoctrinating instead of educating.

If others find this of interest so much the better.

---

[1] Political Class - Individuals, their enablers and hangers on, who believe that their importance, beliefs and abilities require them to tell their fellow citizens how to live their lives.

Understanding the Political Class

CONTENTS

Understanding the Political Class

INTRODUCTION

The material is organized in three main sections:

Know your government – A very brief overview of the roles of our government. The three levels discussed are federal, state and local with an aside on the role of the courts.

Understanding Politicians – Some insights gained over the years regarding the political class's motivations, abilities, and weaknesses,

Free Markets - A quick primer on the advantages of free markets.

Finally I close by providing some suggestions on what you can do to survive and prosper in this environment.

At the end there is a list of additional reading and references if you wish to delve deeper into these issues...

Understanding the Political Class

1 KNOW YOUR GOVERNMENT

The following provides some basic information on the roles of various levels of government, their structure and abilities.

To begin you need to have your own definition of what the role of government is. This definition will change over time based on your own experience and observations. This definition will impact how you view and participate in the political process. A good place to begin is the role of the Federal Government as stated in the US Constitution: 'establish Justice, insure domestic tranquility, provide for the common defense, promote the general Welfare, and secure the Blessings of Liberty to ourselves and our Posterity'. This is a very basic definition that has served us well. However many find it hampering their activities because they wish to do more and you will hear many assertions such as the following:

- To provide for the neediest
- To provide healthcare for all
- To reallocate wealth more fairly
- To protect the weak and downtrodden

An argument can be made for all of these and some countries have tried to incorporate them in their founding documents. The difficulty is that in order to accomplish these goals the government has to increase its power and ability to control and direct it populace, all guided of course by the powers that be, i.e. the political class. And if one objects then one will be labeled 'uncaring', 'mean spirited' and other opprobrious terms. And finally history has shown these altruistic objectives do not achieve their laudable goals they can actually harm the very groups they are trying to assist. For an introduction on this topic see 'Pathological Altruism' in this book and read up from the projects by Walter Williams (in suggested reading).

Basically it comes down to how you prefer to live your life. There are many possible answers ranging from:

> Option 1 - "I want to do what I want with as little interference as possible from the government enjoying the gains and suffering the consequences"

> To:

> Option 2 - "I want to be taken care of and in return will do as the government tells me."

There are many levels in between but understand that if the political class gets its way you will end up in option 2. A more vigorous defense of option 1 is in the Free Market section of this pamphlet.

Federal Level

> Our national government was founded as a republic. It was set up, under a constitution, to provide such common services as might be necessary but curb the excesses that men

would inevitably attempt to impose. Do not let anyone tell you the Constitution is out of date, those that do so inevitably have an agenda that is being thwarted, or at the very least slowed down. The Constitution grants enumerated powers to the government it the basic three branches executive, legislative and judicial while retaining all other powers to the people. The powers do not come from the government but rather from the people who have listed what activities they, the people, have ceded to the government. This approach and structure has proven very effective in keeping a balance and avoiding populist excesses.

A strong argument can be made that pure democracy does not work because it leads to mob rule and the passions of the moment being imposed. The beauty of our form of government is the checks and balances work at tempering the passions of the moment yet allowing good concepts to get agreed on in a measured manner.

I strongly suggest you read The Constitution, and the Declaration of Independence, at least once. Beyond that The Federalist Papers provide a great background on the discussions that lead to the creation of the Constitution, I recommend a modern version which corrects the spelling and language to the English of today.

State Level

Each state government has its own constitution and we will not try and define the differences. They all generally agree on such things as infrastructure building and maintenance, higher education, regulation of common services (such as electricity, gas, etc.) and services for various groups. There are large differences in how they raise money with some having income taxes, some sales taxes, and other fees to raise revenue. Also under the US constitution the states are allowed a great deal of latitude in how they provide these services to their constituents. This allows for a way to test and see what works and what does not work without having it imposed in all the states.

However, it is interesting that the US Constitution guarantees each state a republican form of government. There are some duties proscribed for each state sprinkled across the US Constitution which you must read to find.

Local

Local government is the one that affects you as an individual. It is where this such as grade and secondary education, regulation of local businesses, police, fire and EMT services, waste collection and street signage and lighting are managed. It is most unfortunate that most citizens pay little attention to these until a crisis erupts. I strongly recommend you get involved and understand how your local government works and make an effort to make your voice heard. If you do not then you will get the government they want at a price they decide.

The role of the courts

They exist to adjudicate disputes between parties; the identity of the parties defines the level and type of court. As an example disputes between States are addressed in the Federal Court System, disputes between accused criminals and their victims generally begin in local courts. These can be either at a very local level, think municipal traffic courts, county level, or state level.

Each jurisdiction has its own customs and processes and if you have to use them it is best to have someone, an experienced attorney, knowledgeable in their practices and procedures on your side.

2 UNDERSTANDING THE POLITICAL CLASS

If you are going to knowingly exercise your franchise and participate by voting and supporting a political party you should understand the political class. Some of their defining characteristics are listed below:

- Professional politicians world view is based on their experience, training and exposures
- No politician creates a job. At best they can create an environment that encourages the creation of jobs.
- The 'multiplier' attributed to much government spending is flawed
- Politicians cannot pick winners and losers
- Politicians rig the game
- Ideologies substitute for thought and reason
- Money matters
- They like crises
- They will never admit they were wrong
- They hate to look foolish
- They do think they are better
- Pathological Altruism

I will examine each in the following sections, add some thoughts on free markets and some suggestions on how to use your understanding to more effectively communicate with politicians.

An interesting note is that these characteristics have little to do with the categories that the political class likes to use when discussing us. In this document there is no mention of race, class or gender.

World View

Begin with the fact that the majority of the Congress[2] was educated in the law and their experience is in getting elected, understanding and manipulating public opinion, and horse trading. This means they are ignorant in many matters that they are asked to make decisions about, including ways to regulate economic activities. Additionally most are fueled by ambition and the belief that they are important and must be paid attention to.

Add to this the political environment. Which is characterized by constrained resources, which explains their unceasing efforts to gain more through addition taxes and financing schemes. In the political world if one person gains another loses. This is their life whether they are a local mayor or President. In classic economic terms they live in a 'zero-sum' world. Most have no concept of how real growth can happen. A free market is not 'zero-sum' but rather open ended where one person's gain does not necessarily mean another's loss.

2

https://en.wikipedia.org/wiki/Members_of_the_111th_United_States_Congress

Job Creation

A politician's idea of job creation is to take money from you, the taxpayer, and use it to fund a project, or program which will require the hiring of their friends. This is not creating a job as you might have used that money for other more economically productive purposes.

As an example consider the following. There has been a snowstorm. You have shoveled out but your neighbor across the street (an 80 year old widow) is snowed in. Harry your other neighbor suggests you give him $20 towards shoveling out the poor old gal. Then Harry gets his ne-er-do-well nephew to do the shoveling for $10. The end result the old Widow thinks Harry is a peach, the nephew appreciates the money, and you are out $20. When you confront Harry he says the $10 does not even come close to all the work he put in making things happen and you should appreciate all he has done.

What real job creation is when someone creates a good or service that allows someone else to increase their own productivity. A simple example is the farm plow. A farmer finds purchasing a plow increases the amount of land he can farm, with less effort and resources. So he buys it. The plow manufacturer hires people to make the plows and those jobs are actually jobs that are created. All parties are winners.

Understand that much of the politicians approach is based on parroting what they have heard, or regurgitating talking points they have been given. You also need to realize that their experience is all in taking from one and giving to another. Governments do not create real jobs they can only create an environment that allows jobs to be created.

The 'Multiplier'

You likely have heard mention of a 'multiplier' that magnifies the benefits of various programs. This is based on an assumption that only benefits accrue. In the food stamp example many love to use they go on about how a dollars' worth of food stamps, gets passed on to the store, who pays their suppliers and employee, who in turn spend their part of the dollar on further goods and services. Basically what they are talking about is the velocity of money passing from one to another. Totally ignored in the academic underpinning of this prattle is the negative impact that taking a dollar from someone has. Who is to say what that person might have done with that dollar? They might have spent it on groceries, invested in a great new idea, loaned it to someone else. This money has its own velocity and multiplier which may or may not exceed the programs balancing out any gain. This is not discussed in their literature yet is very real.

Winners and Losers

They believe they can pick winners and losers where neither their experience nor their training provides the basis for this. What actually happens is that their experience leads them to assess a situation and pick a particular approach that suits to their ideology, a constituency or a contributor (which is what lands some of them in jail). Here a few examples and the losses.

> Solyndra $529 Million
> ECOtolity $115 Million
> Fisker Auto $139 Million-

And the losses come from the losses to cronies from things such as the sale of mineral rights on federal lands. You can do your own research and as an exercise try to find equivalent major successes.

Rigging the game

They garner wealth for themselves and their supporters. How? By creating a legal environment that allows them to do so. One CT representative had excess campaign funds which they donated to the state party who in return hired the spouse of the politician as a consultant for most of the 'donation'. All legal but now the politician has increased their net worth with funds that had been donated to help them get elected.

You should ask yourself why a person would want to spend millions to gain a job that pays $125,000 a year.

The push for an increased minimum wage has to be viewed with several things in mind.

1. There is no evidence that increasing it has improved the lot of those receiving it. (i.e. raising them out of poverty) Rather some economists, Walter Williams for one, have documented how an increase harms the classes it aims to help. For more on this go to suggested reading.
2. The unions support this since many public unions have wages that are based on a certain amount over the minimum wage. So an increase in the minimum wage means an increase for their members and in turn an increase in the union coffers.
   As an example see the contract between Service Employees International Union local 32BJ and the Washington Service Contractors Association- Baltimore City http://www.dol.gov/olms/regs/compliance/c ba/box/private/W/Washington%20Service% 20Contractors%20Association- Baltimore%20City%20K9293.pdf Which requires that the minimum hourly wages shall exceed any statutory applicable minimum wage rate by fifty cents. No wonder the union is on the march for an increase in the minimum wage.

The current relationship between certain politicians and Public Service Unions should be of concern since the unions provide votes to those politicians who then in return increase their wages. This is not to say unions do not have a proper place but that is when they are in an adversarial relationship with their opposite. When they and the opposition are in a mutually advantageous relationship then bad things will inevitable happen. With you as their piggybank.

This also is seen in the packing of regulatory bodies and approval of Judges.

And never forget gerrymandering and concept that goes back to 1812 when Governor Elbridge Gerry redrew the Massachusetts State Senate districts to the advantage of those in his political party. The practice continues to this day driven by the decennial US Census which reapportions the numbers of representatives across the states but allows the states to draw up the geography of the districts.

Ideologies trumps ideas

All too many politicians join a party that they think improves their chances of getting elected. Very few join from strong beliefs. However, once joined they have to prove they belong by demonstrating their adherence to the beliefs of the party. That provides cover in one way and also means they do not have to think through issues for themselves, they just collect the talking points and mouth what they are told. As fewer and fewer think through the issues they are coming to increasingly rely on position papers written by others who have agendas of their own. This also leads to an increase in name calling where anyone who disagrees has to be vilified since the politician themselves cannot argue or refute the items under discussion so they must attack on a personal level. Very sad. Observe for yourself how when a new idea is proposed rather than discuss the merits the discussion devolves about how this shows the proposer wants to harm some group or other.

Money matters

There is not much that needs to be said. Realize that since they get what they consider a pittance for their services they are continually in the need of funds for campaigning and other expenses. Those who give them money expect and get something in return or the money dries up.

They like Crises

They love crises as it provides them with a platform to demonstrate their empathy and ability to provide leadership. They have even been known to create crises so then can then impose their 'solutions'.

They are never wrong

They will go to any length to explain why they voted on way or another but notice they do not admit to wrongdoing unless they are caught red handed. Even then they will hope you forget.

They hate to look foolish

This exposes the house of cards they have built.

They do think they are better

The want the trappings of their position and expect recognition of same. Think of the motorcade phenomenon where their passage needs to be clear of riff raff. No consideration is given to the disruption of normal transportation just that they need to get to their destination. Look at the perks they demand for themselves. Think of the full pensions, private barber shops, exclusive lunch rooms and healthcare that Congress arrogates to itself, all with taxpayers money.

Pathological Altruism

Pathological Altruism is championed by Barbara Oakley of Oakland University in Rochester Minnesota published a paper, "Concepts and Implications of Altruism Bias and Pathological Altruism," it is a concept that is just beginning to be noticed and discussed. It is altruism which attempts to promote the welfare of others instead result in unanticipated harm. A crucial qualification is that while the altruistic actor fails to anticipate the harm, "an external observer would conclude [that it] was reasonably foreseeable." Thus, she explains, if you offer to help a friend move, then accidentally break an expensive item, your altruism probably isn't pathological; whereas if your brother is addicted to painkillers and you help him obtain them, it is.

The political class loves to wrap themselves in altruism and empathy, and both have rightly received an extraordinary amount of research attention. This focus has permitted better characterization of these qualities and how they might have evolved. However, it has also served to reify their value without realistic consideration about when those qualities contain the potential for significant harm.

As an example well-meaning governmental policy promoted home ownership, a beneficial goal that stabilizes families and communities. The government-sponsored enterprises Freddie Mac and Fannie Mae allowed less-than-qualified individuals to receive housing loans and encouraged more-qualified borrowers to overextend themselves. Remember Barney Frank saying 'Let's roll the dice'. Look it up. Typical risk–reward considerations were marginalized because of implicit government support. The government used these agencies to promote social goals without acknowledging the risk or cost. When economic conditions faltered, many lost their homes or found themselves with properties worth far less than they originally had paid. Government policy then shifted to the cost of this "altruism" to the public, to pay off the too-big-to-fail banks then holding securitized subprime loans. And then blamed everyone else when the bubble burst. Altruistic intentions played a critical role in the development and unfolding of the housing bubble in the United States.

Want to learn more here is a link to the paper http://www.pnas.org/content/early/2013/06/04/1302547110.full.pdf

This concept is key to understanding the political class, who on the whole, prefers to ignore the complexities and downsides of their pet projects. They believe you are too stupid to understand that there are consequences of acts some of which might be very bad indeed...

3 FREE MARKETS

Watching the events of the past several months I realized that I needed to articulate why free markets work better over the long run compared to the various forms of command economies. Command economies go by many names – Progressivism, socialism, communism, fascism. I do this for my own peace of mind and to better marshal my arguments when ideologues attempt to dominate conversations regarding the economy. By 'work better' I mean organizing human economic activity in a way that maximizes the opportunity for individuals to pursue their goals and improve the overall economy so there is more for everyone. History has shown that free markets are the only way to make a bigger pie for all to share.

My ten reasons can be summarized as follows: (note: The sequence is not relevant as each reason can become of primary importance based on the situation)

1. The closer the action/decision occurs to affected parties the better the action/decision
2. There is more feedback allowing opportunity for modifications
3. There is a greater ability to adapt to change
4. It lessens the impact of ego on the decision/action
5. Dispersed decision making lessens the magnitude of self-serving infrastructures

6. Having multiple decisions/actions going on at once allows for greater chance of success
7. The best way to minimize inequities is to expand opportunity
8. Ideology has little positive impact
9. Failure, when allowed to bite, breeds success
10. 'Fairness' is subjective

Before expanding on the items know there are several inherent assumptions. The first is that the free markets have multiple parties operating within them as buyers and sellers in a competitive environment. Second, there is communication between parties over what works and what does not. Third, the role of government is essential but limited.

1 - The closer the action/decision occurs to affected parties the more likely the action/decision will be good from their standpoint.

> Consider the simple purchase of a loaf of bread. If you go to a local bakery, buy a loaf of bread and it is no good, you have multiple options. The most obvious would be to go back to the store immediately and ask them to make good. If they don't, or even if they do, you will consider going to another store to get bread. If you are removed however from the transaction, for example by having someone else buy your bread, and the bread is bad you will discuss this with the intermediary, who then has to deal with your complaint. They will decide on what course of action to take, which at the very least puts a time lag in the situation. Different factors will creep into the

decision, such as what is the motivation of the intermediary? – Getting you the bread you like best? Getting the cheapest bread possible? Providing a market for his wife's second cousins bakery? The likelihood of satisfaction is inversely proportional to the number of intermediaries involved between the receiver of the good/service and the provider of the good/service.

2 - There is more feedback allowing opportunity for modifications

Continuing with our bread example. Consider the situation where a baker sells all his wares to a distributor who then resells to retailers. Suppose the baker changes the flour he uses. When and how does the baker find out if his customers liked the change, or not? If the baker does not get immediate feedback on the quality of his wares when does he find out? And would it not be easier for him to respond to the impact of the flour change if he knew in hours rather than finding out over time as his business slowly diminishes? Also if there are multiple bakers serving multiple markets it is easier for a baker to make a change.

3 - There is a greater ability to adapt to change

While the successful in any situation will not easily change their ways, new players and or marginally successful players will look to see what new ways they might use to break into a market. If the transactions are defined from on high there will be little if any opportunity to try out new ways, in general it will be discouraged.

4 - It lessens the importance of ego on decisions and actions

> In a free market economy there is little room for ego. Either an approach works or it doesn't. If it doesn't then it either gets changed or the organization sinks. In command economies when a command comes from on high it is followed and if it doesn't work that doesn't matter. Reasons will be created for the failure and this rationale will become the party line. The original command will not be blamed until all other scapegoats are exhausted and even then may remain as holy writ. Think of the current situation and the decisions by the political class that helped bring it about. Are any of them admitting they were wrong? Situations become frozen in place because X wants it so.

5 - Dispersed decision making lessens the magnitude of self-serving bureaucracies

> If there is a healthy competitive market with multiple players there is little use for bureaucracy, however, in a command economy there has to be infrastructure to make sure the commands are being followed. In time the bureaucracy will create its own rules to assure its continued existence. Machiavelli had it right when he said: '*It must*

be remembered that there is nothing neither more difficult to plan, more doubtful of success, nor more dangerous to manage that the creation of a new system. For the initiator has the enmity of all who would profit by the preservation of the old institutions and merely lukewarm defenders in those who would gain by the new ones.'

6 - Having multiple decisions/actions going on at once allows for greater chance of success

Competitive, free markets with multiple players means there are multiple paths being tried at all times, some of which will work, some very well, and some will fail. In command structures alternatives will not be tried instead rewards are given to those who best follow the command strictures.

7 - The best way to minimize inequities is to expand opportunity

There always will be those who receive greater rewards than others, sometimes because of their own efforts, sometimes because of their forbearers, sometimes because of the right connections and sometimes from the luck of the draw. The free market increases the probability that the reason is from the first two not the latter two. There also is a premise on the part of those who believe in command economies that it is a zero sum game and that those who have more have somehow taken it from those who have less. Much of this stems from classical economic theory which still has not learned how to deal with innovation and keeps a focus on capital and labor competing over a limited resource pool. Free markets encourage innovation which makes for a bigger pie which means more for everyone. It is not a zero sum game.

8 - Failure, when allowed to bite, breeds success

There is an interesting tradeoff between encouraging competition, innovation and change and the price extracted when the innovation and change does not work. One needs to encourage competition, reward the winners, but not belittle the losers. On the other side the attitude that it does not matter as long as you tried your best leads to encouraging folks in endeavors where they have no ability. Free markets create an environment that naturally balances this by allowing innovation and rewarding the successful innovator with sales. The failures are quickly shunted aside and those who participated are motivated to move on to different situations. If the failed attempts are allowed to continue they represent a drain on the overall economy and misdirection of resources to a failed enterprise. Those who participated in the failed endeavor will have to find new places to work. For example look at the failed Washington DC education systems and their fight with charter schools. The command structure keeps throwing money at the failed approach and is hostile towards the charter schools despite their improved results with the children and the support of many of the parents. As an aside one might ask where do the children of the command structure send their children?

9 - Ideology has little positive impact

There are many examples of the perversion of economic systems by ideologies. One of the most egregious examples would be Mao Tse Tung's, 'Great leap forward' and the Cultural Revolution. China did not get back on the rails until Deng Xiaoping practically observed – "it doesn't matter if a cat is black or white, so long as it catches mice". There generally is great harm done when an ideology is the motivating factor in implementing an approach. The disruptions are great, the results minimal, and unfortunately scapegoats are found to be the cause not the failed ideology. While I can list many historical examples, a more relevant approach is to recognize those ideologies being used to force solutions on us today. Especially in the name of the environment.

10 - 'Fairness' is subjective

There is a lot of talk about 'fairness' nowadays. You need to remember that 'fairness' is abstract and very subjective and that what is fair is all in the eye of the beholder. Do not allow the term to be used without understanding just what that party means by 'fairness'. A free market does not rely on the term 'fairness'. A free market does not coerce but allows players to decide for themselves what they will sell or buy. Some items will be more in demand and thus gain greater rewards for those who sell them. Also if someone finds a way to create a good or service in a simple, less expensive way, they will make a greater profit and thus be rewarded for their innovation. How is it fair to take from them and give to those who have just sat by?

Having said all that does not mean that government does not have a role to play. It does. The role can summarized as follows:

- Provide a safe and secure environment within which citizens can operate
- Provide a framework for the creation of infrastructure that is used by all
- See that the game is not rigged- a common, agreed upon set of rules that most agree with.
- Provide a framework of laws within which we can operate

In summary, free markets are not perfect but they allow mankind the best chance to secure their inalienability rights to pursue life, liberty and the pursuit of happiness. Command economies do not offer this promise.

4 WHAT CAN BE DONE

What can you do?

If you have gotten this far congratulations!

But now I must warn you that there is little that you can do to change the political class, however, there are some things you can do to minimize the harm they do and even in some cases take advantage of them.

Get involved

Especially at the local level. Meet and understand your mayor, selectman, or whoever is running the place. Depending upon your circumstances you may not be able to do much more, but do as much as you can. Vote. Join the party of your choice and go to their meetings if at all possible. Realize that it takes time for people to trust your judgment and commitment. But this is where you live and you need to do what you can to see that it is run properly. If you do not then you have no grounds for complaint.

I also strongly suggest you consider joining a major party and not a fringe party, even if the fringe party is more representative of your beliefs. Why because, the fringe party, with rare exceptions will not get anything done, except for making themselves feel good. Politics is all about compromise and getting the best you can, not just the best. Why? Because there are many conflicting interests even in the simplest situations and compromise is the way to get something done. Much harm is done in the world by those who force their solutions on the public.

Be careful not to become a member of the Political Class. Be strong. If you do not understand this read 'Animal Farm'.

Do not expect fairness

The right or wrong of a matter is generally not of any concern to the political class as they generally have come to believe that everything is gray and it is all a matter of perspective. So they will gravitate to actions that, in their mind,

- Increases their exposure (i.e. get on TV, etc.),
- is seen to be doing something in a crises – even if it is destructive in the long run,
- benefits a constituency, or donor

Other than that they will smile and move on. It is their nature.

Money matters

They can be bought, or at least made to be sympathetic. You want to have your mayor or congressman pay attention to you? Then either donate to their campaign, or provide a group that you control that can assist them in some way. Unions do both and have influence far beyond their actual numbers.

Vanity, vanity all is vanity

Their ego is all that many have going for them so you may get some traction by appealing to their benevolence and influence.

PC needs to be treated with care

Most are terrified about being not politically correct so if possible position your request as one that complies with current political correctness. You will not get very far, even if you are correct, if your request upends current sacred cows. As an example think of the gun laws that were passed after the Sandy Hook shooting. There was no attention paid to the impact the violent computer games that the shooter played, nor to sad state of mental health capabilities. It was far easier to be seen to do something about those evil guns. Anyone who said otherwise was ignored or publically castigated as uncaring.

You cannot be too cynical

Armor yourself against the political class lack of honor and principle. Most will sell themselves out in a nanosecond it a better offer comes along. Do not expect them to keep their word.

Recognize platitudes

You will hear politicians say all kind of things. A good test to see if the statement really means something. Take the direct opposite and see if any normal rational person would take that position. For example you will hear statements such as 'I am against shootings in our schools' this is clearly a platitude meant to offend no one yet make it seem the speaker is staking out a position on principle. Think of the opposite statement 'I am for shooting in our schools' obviously preposterous which no normal person would say. It will take some practice but identifying those who mouth platitudes will help you identify the panderers.

A caution though, based on my own experience it is best not to confront a platitude mouther as doing so will make them appear foolish (see prior section) and their reaction may be rather extreme.

Beware of assertions

The old saying is: 'Figures do not lie but liars can figure' holds true today. We here every day assertions of one sort of the other such as:

- Salt is bad for you
- We are having an epidemic of X. (you can fill in the diseases and or activities of the moment)
- The ice caps will be gone in Y years.
- A recent study shows that Z is bad for you.

The problem with all of assertions such as these is that they never provide the full back up data or references. Merely by asserting something they expect you to believe. Do so at your peril. I have live long enough to have been subjected to all manner of Armageddon's. The funny thing is that over time they have all been proven wrong. For example the food scare begun by Malthus was reiterated by the Club of Rome in the 1950s, and had it proponents through the 1990's. The green revolution put an end to that. And as far as diets go salt and fats were terrible demonized. The study's upon which these dietary elements were demonized are now being shown to be flawed. Meanwhile much harm may have been done with unintended consequences on the public's health.

Another assertion is a variant of 'The Science is settled'. First off science is never settled as it continually asks questions and questions assumptions. Read any true scientists works and you will find they all question everything. That is the way science proceeds. History is littered with dogmas that everyone agrees were indisputable truths till someone came along and question the assumption. That is why in the reading I included the Feynman book 'The Pleasure of Finding Things Out'.

My best advice is not to live your life in fear and eat a balanced diet.

Douglas A. Nagan

ADDITIONAL READING

F.A, Hayek

The Constitution of Liberty: The Definitive Edition
ISBN 10:0-226-31537-1

This collection of Hayek's writing provides a wonderful basis for understanding the rationale for liberty. If you are a serious student of the political arena and want to be able to discuss the issues involved from a good foundation this is a must read.

Francis Fukiyama –

The Origins of Political Order
ISBN 978-0-374-22734-0

A very intriguing 2 volume set (the second volume is to be published later in 2014) that provides a historical perspective on how, and why, the human animal developed political structures. If you want to understand how we got here this is a very good introduction.

Milton Freedman

Capitalism and Freedom
ISBN 0-226-26421-1

This book provides the definitive rationale for capitalism and why it provides the only way for the majority of people to taste freedom. While Freedman is known as an economist this book provides a sound introduction to why capitalism works as why command approaches fail.

Eric Hoffa –

The True Believer
ISBN 0-06-050591-5

Written by a longshoreman in the 1950's it provides a very powerful indictment against the mindset of the true believer. IF you want to understand the blind adherence of individuals to various ideologies this will provide the basis.

Richard Feynman –

The pleasure of finding things out
ISBN   13-978-0-465-02395-0

If you would like to appreciate how a scientist views the world you should read this. It is a powerful antidote against the belief that science is settled. It never it, it is always about questioning and evolving.

Walter E. Williams -

Up from the Projects – An Autobiography
ISBN 978-0-8179-1255-0

Instead of reading about the race hustlers read this to get a perspective about how a strong minded individual lived through the turbulent times and rose to be a powerful voice for free markets and individual liberty.

Thomas Paine –

Common Sense
ISBN 978-1499-594508

If you want a historical perspective of what the thinking was like when our country was being created this is necessary reading.

Hamilton, Madison & Jay

The Federalist Papers
ISBN 978-1499-709124

A collection of articles promoting the US Constitution during the period of ratification. It provides in the founders words the rational underpinning our founding document. If you want to really understand the US Constitution this is necessary reading. Also make sure you get and read an updated version, such as the ISBN above as the original uses 18th century spelling and grammar which can be off putting to the modern eye..

Douglas A. Nagan

INDEX

Understanding the Political Class

www.ingramcontent.com/pod-product-compliance
Lightning Source LLC
Chambersburg PA
CBHW070405290526
45790CB00004B/1637